Poems of Inspiration for your Soul

Robin Marie Anderson

WESTBOW
PRESS®
A DIVISION OF THOMAS NELSON
& ZONDERVAN

WestBow Press books may be ordered through booksellers or by contacting:

WestBow Press
A Division of Thomas Nelson & Zondervan
1663 Liberty Drive
Bloomington, IN 47403
www.westbowpress.com
1 (866) 928-1240

ISBN: 978-1-5127-4696-9 (sc)

Library of Congress Control Number: 2016910131

Print information available on the last page.

WestBow Press rev. date: 7/11/2016

Contents

Introduction

My poems speak of a unique voice from the ghetto of Chicago.

The poems titled "About Last Night," "Let Go," and "Being There" All speak with an effective use of echoing rain, with love as my main theme.

The poem "What It Takes" traces the history of a long relationship, while the verse "Quiet Little Baby" forms a charming lullaby lyric.

Some struggles and triumphs are revisited in my poem "Reflections" and "A Will Is a Way "demonstrates the power of resolve. The poem titled "Bus Ride" passes through the domain of disenfranchisement, and the verse "Walk with Me Lord' ask for divine guidance. Here are my poems of compelling directness, filled with a spirit of challenge and faith, with much to say about those marginalized, but also about our relationship to God. My poems are also filled with healing and laughter.

I am an African-American who grew up in Robert Taylor Homes on the Southside of Chicago.

I attended Tolton Center March of 1998 and wrote my first poem "My Eyes Don't Cry" and held one of the leading roles in a Drama-Read-A-Rama as Aunt Dew in June.

My poems are based on what I saw growing up as a child and what I have been through in my life. My hope is that my poems will touch the hearts of my readers.

Robin Anderson

Subtitle topic

We all need healing and laughter in our lives.
It takes time to heal, but it takes a second to smile
and tell someone you love them. When I think of
healing and laughter, I feel and think of us all in the world.
We all have lost our love ones. Laughter is good for the soul.
Healing heals us and inspiration up-lift us.

"Learn to take me and me out of yourselves, and
Replace it with us or we, and the world would be
a better place."

Robin Anderson

A Better Place

Somewhere there's a better place
Somewhere there's shinning faces
Somewhere there's sweet smell of flowers
Somewhere there's
A better place
A shinning face
A better race
A better world

A Man

A man will be a man
A man will stay out all night
A man will be a man
No matter what you do
A man will break your heart
And leave you feeling blue
A real man will be a father
A phony man won't even bother
A real man will wipe your tears
And help you get over your fears
A real man will take time to love
Just like a beautiful dove
A real man will stick close
A real man will love you most
A real man will bring you joy
And not act like a little boy
A real man where is he
Where can that real man be?

A Mom

A mom like you
Makes me believe in myself
To me there is no one else
Truthful and kindness
Is a part of you?
Remember some of
Our dreams come true

A Walk by the Sea

One day I was walking by the sea
Talking away with Jesus and me
His spirit came along my heart
I knew we would never depart
I look at the world now
It's not the same somehow
One day we will meet him
Some in hell where
It's dark and dim
He said the flesh is weak
The spirit is willing
Men, women and children going
Around robbing, stealing and killing
I went for a walk by the sea one day
With all of God's people
Walking the same way

A Will Is A Way

A will is way
You just do it
A will is a way
You say it
A will is power
You just believe it
A will is love
You feel it
A will is God
You just read it
A will is a teacher
You just teach it
A will is a doctor
You heal it
A will is a way
You make it
A will is wisdom
You know it
A will is a child
You raise them
So what's your will?

A Woman

A real woman first love herself
A real woman will love her kids
A real woman will love her mate
A real woman knows what it takes
A real woman makes mistakes
A real woman is true to herself
Even if it means being alone
A real woman loves her husband
A real woman cares who she meets
A real woman stays home
And admit when she is wrong

About Last Night

About last night
I'm sorry for what I done
About last night
We were too drunk to have fun
About last night
How did we get home?
It really don't matter
I know you done wrong
About last night
I have to admit
About last night
I don't remember
Please stay off the road
Don't drink and drive

Agree

It's not a good idea
To always agree with some things
Sometimes it's ok
Sometimes it's the wrong way
Some of us care
Some of us don't
Some will and some want
When you agree make sure it's two
When you pray God hears you
We pray for wrong reasons
The Lord don't always agree
How would you know?
If you have been praying
Half of your life and
It's not here he saying no
Agree on good things
And let the bad go

Angel Above

I look at the stars above
Knowing it's you that
I'm thinking of
Let me show you what I mean
Through all of my dreams
Don't give up no matter
How hard it seems
Why not just love
This is why I sing
My song from heaven above
Just because

Anyway

I look at the clouds in the sky and
I often wonder why
The wind blowing in different directions
Some of us cannot be corrected
We go look for trouble
Then it comes back double
We can't go on this way
It hurts I don't know if
You are going to stay
I keep on going anyway

At Night

At night I sit by my window
Watching the moon
For some reason
I found it to be pleasing
I did this for a week
I found strength in that moon
In some kind of way
That's when I knew Christ
Was here to stay
The Lord blesses us all
Whether we are big or tall
He blesses all others to
Whether we are cream, black, or blue
Thank You

Aunts

Some aunts are very loving
Some are very mean
Some have a few some have lots
Call your aunt sometime
They are very kind
They will cry with you
Some don't care if you turn blue
I pray that they will come around someday
And make everything ok
We don't know what they been through
We have to love them always
We all have to go one day
I love all my aunts in every way

Be Determine

Be determine to do good
Feeling sorry for yourself
Is like being a pile of wood
Be determine to treat people right
Let them deal with their own strife
Be determine to love
Like a beautiful dove
Be determine to help someone
One day your blessing will come
Be determine to educate
It's a bad feeling when there is hate
Be determine to love your parents
It' the right thing to do
Be determine to pray for one another
Always love your sisters and brothers

Being There

I wish I was there with you
To hold you when you are blue
One day we will be joined together
I pray we be happy to the end
I see your smile in my dreams
I care for you no matter
How hard it seems
You have been hurt before
I have been hurt a lot more
I see us on a beautiful lake
Praying to our Lord Jesus about our heartaches
I went to God and prayed
Lord Jesus touch us all of
Our heartaches and pain

Bluebird

I see a bluebird
Searching for herself
Calling reaching out
To God for help
She prays night and day
She reaches out to her children
This bluebird keeps on going
No matter what folks say?
She know she have wings and
She can fly away
Sometimes bluebirds fall
Until the Lord gives her a call
This is the end until I meet thee
By the way that bluebird is me

Breakthrough

In life we have troubles
Sometime it hurts double
I am beginning to believe
We must hurt and bleed
Not in a bad way
If we don't hurt
In our lives
We won't have anything to say
I have been hurt
A lot in my life
I say thank you Lord
My breakthrough is coming
When it does
I will take off running

Bridge Over Troubled Waters

I pray for all who lost
Their loved ones to
Wars, earthquakes, tornados
Guns, fires, hurricanes, and sickness
I'm talking bridge over troubled waters
We take life for granted
In a flash we could be gone
Sometimes things happen
To bring the world closer
Let's face it God is near
I'm talking bridge over troubled waters
I hold no grudges or un-forgiveness
No hatred, I love everyone
When I am gone, I have told you
I'm talking bridge over troubled waters
There is no greater love
Then Jesus Christ our Lord
When we are gone
We have to cross
That bridge over troubled waters
Before we get to our final resting place
We have to cross that
Bridge over troubles waters

Broken

Broken marriages brings broken children
Broken homes brings broken families
Broken promises brings broken dreams
Broken glass brings broken streets
Broken laws brings a broken nation
Broken hearts brings a broken man
Broken pain brings broken gain
Broken laws brings broken government
Lord Jesus forgive us all only
He can fix our broken pieces

Brothers

A brother sometimes don't come around
To talk to him you have
To search all over town
To all of you who have a brother
They are like no other
Just because he's not around
If you search hard enough
He can be found
You bother big sister
He will talk it through
You mess with little sister
I feel sorry for you
When he doesn't call
Brothers have downfalls
If you call your brother sometimes
He will tell you why men act a fool at times
Love your brother in everyway
My brothers are fun everyday

Building a Foundation

One day while thinking in my chair
A friend of mine came out of nowhere
She had lots of big dreams
She begin to write all kind of things
She wanted fancy cars and rings
She wanted a big fine house
She said, girl what do you think?
I said, flush them down the sink
You forgot what you missed
How can buy anything?
First you have to figure out the cost
If you don't you will be lost
Now you can build your foundation

Bus Ride

I ride the bus some days
Always praying for sunshine
To come my way
I see things to make me wonder
My heart goes out to hunger
I get off the bus and
The homeless asking for dimes
As the years go by its harder times
I see disrespect of children today
I pray that Jesus would come their way
Some bus rides are sad to see
A bus ride can be fun for you and me

Call on Jesus

Call on him through hard times
Call on him when you don't have a dime
Call on him when you need a friend
He will hear your call to the end
Call on him just to call
He always gives his all in all
Call on him in everyway
Say Jesus and watch all things go
Your way just like you prayed
Let's call on him everyday

Chance

What if you had a chance?
To do everything you can
What would it be?
You can make the water cleaner
The trees and grass greener
Build a shelter for the homeless
Build homes for seniors
Spend time with them
You can heal the sick
You can feed the hungry
No one will ever be lonely
Jesus was not bought for a cost
So live your life while you can
Until you meet the Father of all
Are you ready for your call?

Christians

We all want to be Christians
We all have our say in being one
We say I'm filled with the spirit
We go to church on Sunday
Go drink on Monday
Curse on Tuesday
Gossip on Wednesday
Tell a lie on Thursday
Fornicate on Friday
Try to overcome on Saturday
Remember only one is perfect

Color

What color am I?
I'm very bright
My color you can see at night
God made me this way
So why should I go astray
What color am I?
I'm very dark
I wear bright clothes so
You can see me in the park
Just remember I have a heart
What color am I?
I'm brown skin
Maybe I could be thin
In life I want to win
Whether we are black, brown, or blue
God sees all of us like he see you
Why kill and fight over color
We all bleed the same
That's a shame

Come Together

No more restless nights
Our Lord Jesus is always right
To all my family and friends
We must come together
Life is not forever
We can't hold grudges
We must let them go
None of us know
Which way God wind blows?
Let's love another
And forgive and let's live

Cousins

Cousins are loving and kind
Some are very understanding
Some of them don't come around
Some will tell you were to go
Some talk it out
Some of them you don't hear from
You be wondering
What have I done?
We all should love our cousins and
Pray for them in everyday
Let's love cousins
I mean this in everyway

Cry Freedom

World, can you see
What they done
To you and me
Cry Freedom!
Planes, people crashing DC
Trade Center blasting
People jumping from high floors
Burning, crying, running through doors
Our people cry, "Freedom!"
Our babies cry, "Freedom!"
No one was looking for this
Planning this was not right
This will be a whale of a fight
How could you kill so many?
Did you think about you had any?
Cry Freedom is what you did
Did you think of your kids?
Cry Freedom!
Kids, teenagers are scared
This was a terrible threat
Something you will regret
Cry Freedom!
Our sons and daughters go to war
No more blood and burning no more
This just doesn't make any sense
Cry Freedom!
The world will never forget this day
9-11 year 2001 when the world went astray
Cry Freedom! This is world history

All this mess was misery
Cry Freedom!
Is what we cry
Cry Freedom-many lives lost
Cry Freedom-many lives saved
Never anything like this
That happened to the world today
Cry Freedom Cry
Cry Freedom what
The world cry

September 12, 2001 11:30 a.m.

Daughters

I love my daughters in everyway
They grow up and move away
Mother's be there to tell them
Girl if you don't stop
Moms are not always right
We are not always wrong
This is why we preach to your
That same old song
Listen to your mom
No matter what she is?
Listen to her no matter what she did
We have been there and done that
This is why you get trapped
We know you have to grow up
And you will leave home
This is why our door is always open
When things go wrong
I love all of you
And the baggage that
You bring when a man hurts you

Mother's be there to tell them

Girl if you don't stop
Moms are not always right
We are not always wrong
This is why we preach to your
That same old song
Listen to your mom
No matter what she is?
Listen to her no matter what she did
We have been there and done that
This is why you get trapped
We know you have to grow up
And you will leave home
This is why our door is always open
When things go wrong
I love all of you
And the baggage that
You bring when a man hurts you

Do What the Spirit Says

Do what the spirit says
You have to sit quiet sometimes
You can hear him say
Come to me you're mine
Do what the spirit says and
Things will begin to happen
Don't listen to a fool
One wrong move
You will miss your blessings
Sometimes He takes years
Sometimes He takes seconds
Do what the spirit says and
You will not miss your blessings

Dreams

One night while lying in bed
Visions of beautiful light in my mind
I saw an image of a man
He was walking across the promise land
He spoke to me in a peaceful voice
He said my child you will be
A gift to the world one day
All of a sudden he went away
I know this vision will be with me always
I know I will have good days

Dumb and Slow

One day there was a little girl
She helped everyone she could
Just because of her reactions
She was called dumb
Just because of the way she talked
She was always called slow
This little girl always wondered
Why some wanted to follow
Her everywhere she goes
Now let's clarify the word dumb
A dumb person can't read or write
This little girl would stand and fight
A slow person is someone who
Is mentally dull and lacks speed
This little girl came a long way
She keeps on moving everyday
Everyone who called her slow
What it was they didn't know
Some of them are in the same
Place from years ago
By the way that little girl is me
God opened my eyes now I see

Ego

Someone with an ego
Is too far gone
Some get millions
Some get billions
Next thing you know
It's all gone
What happened to me you say
All of sudden your money and
Your ego is taken away
Now you have nothing
If you have a ego
Get rid of it
Or pay the price
Of being a misfit

Father's Day

My father left us years ago he
He left us with things we should know
He bought us up to love everyone
Today that's hard for some
Growing up with a father
Was a blessing to us?
To all the fathers who are feeling blue
Mothers we don't have a clue
What fathers have to go through?
To all who have lost their father?
Don't feel like
You don't have a friend
Talk with our heavenly Father
He will not make times harder
Our father watches over us
Not because he wants he must
He loves all of you
The little babies to
I pray these words I wrote
Will give you a bundle of hope
Happy Father's Day
Happy father's Day
To our loving spiritual Father
Your daughter Robin

Fathers

Fathers are strong
Fathers are bold
Fathers are God's gift to us
Fathers need help like we do
Let's love our fathers in everyway
We never know when
God will call them home to stay
Let's love our Fathers everyday

Feelings

Feelings come and go
Feelings sometimes make us cry
Feelings sometimes make us sad
Feelings make us mad
Feelings of hurt in pain
Feelings come when it rains
We all have different kind
Of feelings everyday
Feelings can make us joyful
Before you talk to someone
And raise your voice
Think about your feelings
It's your choice

For Every Heartbeat

For every heart beat
I feel you far away
Wondering if my sweetheart is ok
Your voice over the phone
The laughs in what we say
For every raindrop that falls
From the sky
My love for you is
The reason why
For every heartbeat and
The sun that shines
I know that you are forever mine
I will hold you and not let go
I pray for our loved ones
And every day we share
I thank our Father above
For he gave us both love

Get On the Train

Get on the train
Don't use the Lord Jesus
Name in vain
Get on the train
Don't get caught in the rain
Get on the train don't you quit
Don't get caught at being a misfit
Get on the train
It's the right thing to do
God says come as you are
All Gods' people come from near and far
We have to stay on the train
To become all we can be
We can walk side by side
Come everyone and get on this train ride

God Loves Us

One day we love
One day we hate
One day we leave
One day we achieve
One day we steal
One day we kill
One day we hurt
One day we're in pain
One day we're in vain
God loves us all the same

God's Angels

Jesus born lying in a manger searching
The world finding angels
Jesus love with his grace
Forgiving his people not the race
Sinners all over the earth
A beautiful star appeared at his birth
Jesus said come me if you need rest
Satan tried to please him with a test
He comes sometimes in our sleep
With pure clean waters ever so deep
I see visions of war all in my mind
Our people doing bad things of all kind
A lot of us who don't believe
There are some who deceive
Walking with Jesus is so divine
He cured the sick, lame and the blind
These are the last and evil days
I pray to you Lord Jesus
Keep us with your ways
He created all things on earth
Women bearing pain giving birth
Jesus said I will not let you thirst
He who comes last comes first
You're not happy with a little
How can I give you more?
Jesus blesses everyone
We all want to hear well done
He warns us in some kind of way
We ignore him living in our selfish ways

We say why me
We first have to seek thee
All of our words have power when we speak
We have to put our pride aside
And pray on our knees
I wrote this with Jesus help there is
No way could I have thought of this by myself
He said knock and I will open the door
Don't over knock I will answer anymore
Peace on earth good will to men
Lord peace to everyone
To all my brothers and sisters in Christ
We will all wake up in paradise
Let's fight for what's right

Grandkids

I love all of you with all of my heart
Right now times are hard
When it's my time to go away
Remember me and my loving ways
Tell stories about me to your kids
Tell them of all my love today
Keep the Lord in your hearts
He will never depart from you
He will give you what you need
Because you are his seeds
After you have lived your lives for Jesus
Remember you will have the best gift of all
A crown is what you'll receive
Live your lives and achieve
Please stay humble no matter what you do
The good suffer with the bad until
Your life is through
Love Grandma

Have You Ever

Have you ever been on the other side?
Have you ever been on a train ride?
Have you ever been poor?
With your rich money and
Your big head pride
Have you ever sat down to think?
How would you feel on the other side?

Hear Me

Can anyone hear me?
Lying in this bed
I am not young anymore
My kids have gone and left me here
In this old bed by myself
My bones are hurting
My body aches
I lie in this bed
With these bones of mine
I am glad when I awake
I want to see my family
My kids and friends
I have lain here for so long
I want to go home
Where I am I get cold
Who will take care of me?
Now that I am old
My Lord hear my cry
Tears rolling down my eyes
And these old bones of mine

Help Somebody

Help Somebody
It's the will of God
Help Somebody
Don't make their way hard
Help somebody
It makes you feel better
Help Somebody
You receive grace
Help Somebody
Run their race
Help Somebody
With a smile on your face
Help Somebody
Don't say it's a disgrace
Help Somebody
To love all over the world
Help our children most of all
Please don't let them fall
Help Somebody

Help

You judge me by what you hear
No proof just the law
I say I'm innocent
You say I'm guilty
Some use their authority
And their power
The good suffer with the bad
Let's face it
It's not going away
Jesus said in his word
They persecuted me
They will persecute you
Help us Lord
Keep us safe
All this war
All this hate
Help me to redeem myself
Rescue me
Set me free
I said my innocent
I said my plea
Lord Jesus help us please
I pray to thee

Home Wrecker

What is a home wrecker?
A home wrecker is
A person without a life
They keep up strife
Their lives is so messed up
They have the nerve to tell
You good luck
When it's all said and done
The home wrecker is the lonely one
I tell you this
If you have a life
Stay away from the home wrecker
And their dirty strife
Let them be the lonely one for
The rest of their life

How Would You Feel

How would you feel?
If you were in my shoes
How would you feel?
If you knew how much pain
I have endured
I wish you could be me
Just for one day
You will understand why
I feel this way
Everyone have good them
We bring out the bad
We are scorn, torn for life
Then we say what happen
To him/her you don't know
The details you add
You take away and assume
How would you feel?
If you were in my shoes

Hurricane

City here all beautiful today
Hurricane, tornados blew it all away
Help them oh Lord
Touch and bless them all
This was very sad and heart felt
Bodies, dirty-water nothing to drink
No time to think
Some of us we are very blessed
We do not know it
We complain about what
We don't have
They have not half
My heart and prayers go out to all
We gossip and some boast
Back to money, gas and war
Now we all are going through
This could have been me or you
God Bless you all

I Am Human

You may think I am strong
I am weak and
I am only human
I make mistakes sometimes
Please forgive me
I am only human
I am not perfect
I have no more or less
I love everyone
Everyone will not love me back
I am only human
All I have been through
Our Lord Jesus loves me
He created me, he knows me
I am only human

I Arose

The stars in the night
My heart broken again
My eyes cry when it rains
I ask the Lord why so much pain
I want to fly and be free
When you seem so far away
I love you always
My hands are warm and true
You left me feeling blue
Where do we go from here?
I know the shepherd is near
I arose and it was he
I arose and
I'm free to be me

I Gave My All

I gave my all just
To take a fall
You told me where we stand
We don't have a second chance
The chance you had you blew it
You broke my heart
All the way through
I'll get back up no matter
What you say or do
Never again will
I fall for you
I gave my all

I Look

I look at the clouds in the sky
And I often wonder why
The wind blowing in different directions
Some of us can't be corrected
We go and look for trouble
It comes back double
We can't go on this way
It hurts I don't know if
You are going to stay
I keep on going anyway

I Sit

I sit in my window
And look at the sky
I say Lord my, my
I sit in my chair
And think about our love ones
Most of them are gone
I see a beautiful rainbow
At the end of it is
A pot of God's gold
I sit by my window and see
The birds free
I say Lord help me please

I Stood Alone

I stood alone
A vision went across my eyes
I was so hurt
Never understood or questioned
All I know I became wise
I stood alone
I had a lot of love around me
Don't go to sleep angry
In peace stand alone
Sometimes in what you do stand alone
Whatever you have been through
Stand alone
We are not alone because
Our Lord Jesus
Stands with you

I Talked

One day in the early morning
My eyes felt stormy
I went to my prayer closet
I begin to open my mouth
I talked with Jesus
I cried unto him
He went to the Father
After I prayed I didn't feel bothered
He bought me out of a situation
I prayed with all my heart and soul
He gave me conformation
I want to thank you Lord
For all you have done
I shouted victory, victory
I have won

I Think

I think of you night and day
For every star in the sky
I imagine you go by
For every flower
That grows each day
I pray for you in everyway
For every tree that stand
I know you are a good man
For every step I take
I know you are my mate

I Want to Be Happy

Lord I want to be happy
My life have been hurt and pain
I want to be happy and not hurt
When it rains
I want to be happy
I want someone to love me
For whom I am and not
Tell lies to get in my pants
I want to be happy after all
I have been through
It seems that special someone
Tell me that he love me
End up running away
When I speak my plea
My temple means a lot
Until you are my husband
You need to stay inside your box

In The morning

In the morning when I awake
I feel good no matter what it takes
In the morning I hear the birds sing
Sometimes they flap their wings
In the morning I know
That God is near
In the morning what's
There to fear
In the morning what will it be?
Two little angels watching over me

Its Harvest Time

Harvest time we plant
Harvest time we grow
We are Jesus seeds
Jesus gives us more
Stand still and know
Harvest time is not hate
Enter his kingdom through
The narrow gate
The road is wide
We must stay inside
Jesus said many go away
Only a few stay
Let's be strong and praise
And sing our song
Harvest time is near
We know that Jesus is here

It's Time

Its time to come home
It's not time to be alone
It's time to love
It's with God above
It's time to laugh
It's time to praise
It's time to give
It's time to live
It's time to create
It's not the time to hate
Bless God's people
All over the earth
For he preached and lived
He died for our sins we should
Thank him every day we live

Jealousy

What is a jealous person?
How can you tell?
A jealous person has no life
They also keep up strife
You can catch them between lines
Listen to what they say at times

Jessie

I knew this man name Jessie
He was there for everyone
He was a good brother to some
He was a good crabby man
When he saw something wrong
He would try to fix it
Just with his kind words
Jessie was always heard
He would feed anyone
All was welcome to come
I remember Jessie, his loving heart
Jessie worked very hard
We all cried when he left
Everyone started thinking about themselves
Jessie was a good man you see
That crabby old man was father to me
We love you Dad
We miss you

Jesus Christ

J is for he gives us justice
E is for eternal life he fills our cup
S is for salvation he freely gives
U is for his undying love
S is for his strength of a dove
C is for the cross he died for us
H is for the world in his hands
R is for we must repent
I is for his inspiration
S is for we all need strength
T is for trails we all go through

Jesus Help

You do not have to accept me
All I need is Jesus to help me see
Please do not call me with your mess
Your mess brings stress
We sometimes down one another
We need each other
Sisters and brothers at each other throat
How can we tell our children how to cope?
Our parent's did not teach us this way
This is what man wants us
To kill each other in everyway
Jesus says love one another
And forgive everyone
We all have our time when he comes

Judge

Some of us judge
And don't know why
Just remember where
You come from
Watch what you say
When you judge
We get on our feet and say
You do this and that
Never thought about what you done
So before you talk about anyone
Why do we judge?
When we don't judge ourselves
Just remember how far you came
Sit and think of yourself
Before you judge someone else

Keep It Moving

Keep it moving
Like you did before
I tried to care for
You all I can
You're not a man
I don't have time for boys
I can play games by myself
Remember you are
The one who left
Keep it moving

Kids

Kids are precious and full of joy
Whether it's a girl or boy
Kids like to have fun
And play games
Some kids make it to fame
Kids have dreams like we do
They don't understand like you
Kids do all kinds of things
Kids are peaceful
Some have troubles
Where are the kids' mothers?
We must come together as caring adults
Not let them fall of feel discussed
We must teach them well or
They will end up in jail

Lady Bug

Lady bug lady bug
Crawling up my window
Orange and pretty
With black spots
Oh how beautiful
I wish you could stay
Fly away fly away

Let Go

Let me go
For I don't know
Let me go
My own way now
Let me go
You have to make
Your own way somehow
Let me go
I say enough is enough
Let me go
Don't do me in
Let me go I will win
Let me go
If I come back
For I know
We are on the same track
Let me go
To fulfill my dreams
Let me go
No matter how hard it seems
Let me go

Let Me Live

Lord let me live for this day
None of us knows when
You will come our way
Let me live for freedom calls
My heart cries for
The world behind the walls
Lord let me live upon this race
Why don't they understand?
We live by grace
Lord let me live to fulfill my dreams
You pick us up along the streams
Lord let your light shine upon my face
Let my heart burn for heaven sake
Lord let the nations come together
Lord you said the world would end
And your words are forever
Lord I feel hurt and pain
By your way we all gain
Lord let me live to see another day
When someone dies my day seems gray
Oh Lord I know you are there
To comfort us all you can bare
Lord you said love one another
Whether we are purple, black pink, or yellow
We are all sisters and brothers
Lord thank you for loving me
For loving us all even though we live
You must give us a call
Until you come for us
We have to live on love, faith
Grace, patient, and trust
Thank you Lord Jesus
For letting me live let me live

Let's Come Together

Let's come together
The world is so messed up
We still have racism to this day
Our love ones fighting war
Turn on the news everyday
Our love ones dying
Let's come together
We must love
It hurts me so
We all must go
Help us Lord Jesus
What can we do?
They don't understand
We all can't get to the promise land
Wake up world please
Everything we do he sees

Love You

I love you in the morning
I love you in the noon
I love you at night
I love you like the bright stars
I love when times are hard
I love you when it seems we are apart
I love you today and always
I love in May
I love you when it rain
I love you because
You took away my pain

Love Yourself

You did all you can do
For family and friends
You suffered for them
You feed them
You bathed them
You hurt with them
You laughed with them
You shared their dreams
You lift them up
You say what is missing
Love yourself
Then you can love everyone else

Marriage

Some of us are
Mislead when it
Comes to marriage
God said a woman
And man should be
Joined together and
Leave his mother and father
God also said honor
Thy mother and father
He did not say disown
And mistreat your parent's
Some of us forget where
We come from and
Mistreat our love ones
And not know
We dislike others
God said love one another
Just as I have loved you

Marriage

Some of us are
Mislead when it
Comes to marriage
God said a woman
And man should be
Joined together and
Leave his mother and father
God also said honor
Thy mother and father
He did not say disown
And mistreat your parent's
Some of us forget where
We come from and
Mistreat our love ones
And not know
We dislike others
God said love one another
Just as I have loved you

Mind over Matter

A mind is very powerful
A strong mind is not doubtful
That's mind over matter
Your friends offer you drugs
That's matter over mind
A true friend will give you a hug
That's mind over matter
Kids stay in school
Don't be no one's fool
That's mind over matter
Tell someone to have a good day
That' mind over matter
Your brother or sister goes astray
You cried, tried, and prayed
Let them make their own way
That's mind over matter
Some folks think you are crazy
That' matter over mind
You call on the name of Jesus
That's mind over matter
The world don't mind
So why should it matter

Misery Love Company

If you are on the right track
Here come someone trying
To knock you on your back
Misery Love Company
Some say they are happy for you
They just saying it on the outside
On the inside you are all kind of things
Misery Love Company

Miss Home

I miss home day by day
Always praying to go home one day
There's no place like home
Whether near or far
The stars in the sky are different
It don't rain the same
You miss all those fun and games
Cuddling and laughing with mom and dad
Sometimes home can be sad
We have to keep on going everyday
We all miss home in some kind of way

I Miss You

My nights are growing colder
My lips long for your kiss
My ear awaits your whisper
My hands long for your touch
My eyes want to meet with yours
Our talks over the phone
Our laughs in what we say
A minute seems like hours
The days seems like years
When will you hold me?

Mistakes

So many have made mistakes
So much a man can take
We live we multiply
We kill, we die, we hurt, and we suffer
We still fight over color
Families so far apart
Times are hard
We need one another
Our children go to war
Governments, politics, leading
Our world today
Our brothers and sisters in prison
Some are innocence
Yet the guilty get away
Lord Jesus bless us all
We always call on him
When we fall
A lot of us still practice hate
Narrow is the road, wide is the gate
Remember we all make mistakes

Mom

If could sail across the water
For all you did for me
You cared for us all
Some of us were blind to see
For every blue wave
It's for the love you gave
For every cloud
You never let us down
For every whisper of the wind
You were there over and over again
These words represent all that
I wish I can do
To sail your troubles away
Your heartaches and pain
Your tears and sorrow
If I could take your hands
My legs whatever pain
Going through your body
I would give it to you
In a moment or seconds
You don't have to ask question
Mom your light will always shine
We love you
We miss you

Money

Money can't buy love
Some of us think so
Money can't buy happiness
Yet some pay for it
Money can't buy dreams
Yet we dream of it
That's what the world is in
Money is the root of all evil
When our love one dies
We fight over it
Some buy their way out with money
Money is easy to borrow
It's hard to pay back
We do need money to survive
Everything in this world
Is lent to us
Our family, spouses, and friends
It's not ours anyway

Mother's Day

A mother is a lady full of precious joy
A mother has lots of pain
A mother will hide her feelings
A mother will not let you down
Children love your mother
No matter how she is
Please remember mother went
Through labor and pain
To get you here
A mother is there always to listen
Love your mother everyday
Call your mother if she
Is far away
When mother is gone
You will feel very alone
Always take time to go back home
God said honor thy father and mother
Some of us don't even bother
Happy Mother's Day to all

My Eyes Don't Cry

My eyes cried at birth
My eyes cried as a kid
My eyes cried growing up in CHA
My eyes cried looking at the homeless
My eyes cried looking at
The children without a mother/father
My eyes cried for hunger in the world
My eyes cried going through abuse
My eyes don't cry
I came a long way in life
My eyes don't cry
I love everyone
My eyes don't cry
When God sends for me
My eyes will not cry
To all my family and friends
Please don't let your eyes cry
We should teach the children
The right way to go
They will never depart
My eyes don't cry
Love to all

My Friend

When things go wrong
I'm still your friend
When I don't have anything to give
I'm still your friend
When you need someone to talk to
I'm still your friend
When I rise in the morning
I'm still your friend
When you feel sad or sorrow
I'm still your friend
When you turn your back on me
I'm still your friend
When you need a helping hand
I'm still your friend
Why do I write and say these words
Because Jesus is my Friend
I have a friend in him
I am a friend
My friend
Love and not Hate

My Heart Torn

You tore my heart into pieces
You told me all these beautiful things
You said I will not hurt you
After all you know what
I have been through
My Heart Torn
I hide my feelings so
No one will know
Only God knows my heart
You said you love me
I need love in my life
My Heart Torn
Someday you will be
In the same situation
The way you hurt me
Someone will do to you and
Your heart will be torn
And you will feel
The pain I endured

My Love for You

My love for you
Is big as the sea
My joy for you
Is big as a volcano
My heart was empty
My joy was sad
My smile was unseen
You came along and fulfilled my dreams
My love for you
Is big as the river flows
My love for you
Is stronger than you may know
My love for you is everlasting
I thank our Lord Jesus
For sending you my way
When you hold me in your arms
I know everything will be ok
Thank you for being pure
I know our love is for sure
Thank you Lord Jesus
For what you have done with
You on our side
We have won

                    To the one I Love

My Window

I look out my window
I look up at the sky
I see a rainbow
I think us all
Who have been through?
I look out my window
I pray the Lord's will
We must let him in
He took all of our pain
He died for our sins
My windows are all colors
I love my sisters and brothers

Nephews

Nephews are very loving
It's hard to catch them at times
I love all of mine
They listen to you sometimes
When the talk is over
They disappear in a flash
They move quickly
They have heartaches like we do
They hurt by themselves
They won't tell you
Some have too much pride
Let the Lord be your guide
If you need me
I will be there by your side

Nieces

A niece is someone who
Looks up to her aunt
A niece will talk with you
Niece's make mistakes to
They are very loving in kind
To all of my nieces let your light shine
You are all friends of mine
Some of us have a lot
Some of us have a few
I tell you love your niece like
She loves you

No Guns

What is the world coming to?
Kids, teens, robbing, shooting, and killing
What's the reason over nonsense?
Need to be in school getting some education
Learning about our history proclamation
Instead parents, grand-parent's in misery
Wondering if my child coming home today
Or is my child gone away
Turn on the news everyday
Instant kids, babies, and seniors dying
While our hearts are crying
Why make things worse than they are
How can we have a better future or
A brighter day knowing
What you did was wrong
I tell you this remember
The gun is in your hand not
Your friend or buddy
Fathers, Mothers let's get a hold of our kids
I wish they had the parents we did
When it's all said and done
You still have to run
Let's put down guns and see
A brighter day

No More

Why does it take for our
Love ones to pass away
Enemies, families and friends
Come together just for that day
God knows what's best
It was our love one time to rest
No more suffering
No more pain
No more crying in the rain
You did all you can do
No matter what it was?
You were always there
No matter how old we get
We think our love ones
Will be with us forever
This is not the case
This is why Jesus gives us
Our own space

No One Believe

No one believe in you
No matter what you do
You go to friends for help
They laugh because they out for themselves
No one believe in you
What do you think?
If it's up to them don't care
If you turn pink
No one believe in you
You sit and cry alone sometimes wish
You would have stayed home
We all one day have
To be on our own
When you are feeling blue
There is only will give you a chance
I tell you this don't go to a man
Go to the one who will
Always see you through
That's God almighty
He keeps on loving you

One Day

One day I was moving around
Mommy took me all over town
This fine day
I knew I would have my way
This day I came into the world
Daddy was there joyful
Whether I was a boy or girl
I love mommy and daddy
I love everyone
Thank you Lord Jesus
For letting me be born

Our Hearts

When we seek God
With our hearts
And stand not be notice
When we knock at the door
He knows when we are true
God makes all of his followers
Leaders from the bottom we start
We prosper in everything we do
I am a living walking, testimony
When we praise and sing
He pours out blessings
We don't have enough room
To receive them

Picture

Look at a picture of yourself
What do you see?
Think about your pain
Think about someone else
Think about how would
Your love one feel
Think about all the folks in the world
Picture their suffering
Picture their broken heart
Picture their parent's tears
Picture how hard we raised them
We did the best we could
Look at your picture and
You will see through it
That picture it could be
You and me
Look at your picture
What do you see?

Please

Please don't turn away
From me dear Lord
Guide us with your love
Believe in him
Humble yourself in his ways
He promised us eternal life
And we live years and years
With our Lord Jesus
Why should we fear?

Praise the Lord

We rejoice with joy
All the girls and boys
Praise the lord
We dance and clap
Praise the Lord Jesus
We praise him when we sing
We know he died for all of everything
Lord let the heavens ring
Praise the Lord

Precious One

Your eyes light like
A star in the sky
Your hand is soft
Like a cloth
Your nose round
Cute and firm
Your skin soft
And gentle just
Like your mouth

Proud To Be Me

Why look at me
And judge me
By what you see
Why throw me behind bars
And say what I did
What happens when it's your kids?
Why do you take and never give
Why look at my color and say
I don't deserve to live
Why say you love me and go away
Leave me bare and lonely because
You can't have your way
Look at me what do you see
I see different colors and say it's me
I raise my hands and pray on my knees
Always from my heart
Through the years I live
And every day I breathe
I'm proud to be whoever you see
Because Jesus Christ created me

Quiet Little Baby

Quiet little baby count your sheep
Quiet little baby go to sleep
Quiet little baby mother is here
Quiet little baby daddy is near
Quiet little baby God loves you
Quiet little baby he loves us to

Reflections

I look in the mirror and I see
Reflections of hate
Reflections of hurt
Reflections of disappointment
Reflections of abuse
Reflections of suffering
Reflections of joy
Reflections of peace
Reflections of love
Reflections of tears
Reflections of me
Most of all
I see reflections of
The light of God

Remember

I was just passing by
I could not tell you all because
I know how hurt
You would have been
Jesus called me by name
Come here my love one
Come nearer take my hand
You are tired you need rest
Christ Jesus knows what's best
I pray for all
This was God's call
I'm sorry I couldn't stop by
I am very sorry for the quick goodbye

Robin Anderson

R is for reality
O is for obedience
B is for beautiful
I is for inspire
N is for natural
A is for angel
N is for nourish
D is for dedicated
E is for exciting
R is for respectful
S is for sensational
O is for orderly
N is for nourish
Please give yourself credit for
all you have accomplished
in your life.

Run On

Have you ever felt sad?
Like the whole world is against you
Walking around with your head down
Some folks looking at you with a frown
I tell you to run on
Have you ever had friends and family members?
You helped them they don't remember
Then here they come again
After years and years
I tell you to run on

Seasons

There are reasons for every season
Winter comes clouds are gray
Snowflakes fall here to stay
That is what we all think sometimes
Spring comes in early march
Beautiful leaves growing from the start
Now here come summer
The sun hot and shinning
Kids at the beach some all tiny
Fall comes and leaves falling off trees
We have summer, spring, winter and fall
Remember God is over them all

Sister-in-Laws

A sister-in-law is
Just like a sister
Sometimes they feel
Out of place
Sometimes they need
Their own space
They also have problems
Just like we do
When it's all said and done
Some of them can be fun

Sisters

A sister is someone
You can talk to
They sometime don't
Like what you go through
You try to ask them
One little simple question
She gives you this talk
On some long lesson
I called my sister
On the phone
Her first question
Is now what's wrong?
For all the people
In the world
You know big sister
Is some king of girl?
A sister is someone
Who really cares?
A sister will always be there

Smile

Smile it makes someone day
They might be feeling gray
Give someone a hug
It makes them feel loved
Tell someone you love them
Their heart won't feel dim
Smile and say thank you
It's the right thing to do
Call a love one right away
We never know when
It maybe our day
Smile, smile everyone
You get a smile back
Your day will be fun

Some Point in Time

Sometimes we take life for granted
Sometimes we cry
Sometimes we laugh
Sometimes we forgive
Some point in time we live
Some point in time we must forgive
Some point in time we must rest
Some point in time we do our best
Some point in time we must die
Some point in time only
Our Lord Jesus knows why

Sons

Sons are very difficult at times
They have too much pride
They worry a lot about mom
They do everything they can
They need their dads
Mother's we can't do dad job
We can calm them and give advice
Every son needs their dad or
Father figure in their lives
Sons get lonely sometimes
That is where dad comes in
And show them the right way to go
Sons please love your dad
No matter how hard it seems
They have feelings like you do
Love them and see them through

Stand Alone

Never leave anywhere or
Go to sleep angry
Go in peace no matter what it is
Sometimes in what you do
Stand Alone
When you talk confess you sins
Don't worry about the consequence
You will win
I stood alone
A vision went across my eyes
This day I was very hurt
I never understood
Nor did I question
After all you been through
Our Lord Jesus stands with you
You are never alone
We all have to go back home

Sunshine

As the sunshine and
The skies are blue their
Is only one man like you?
Your eyes light up
Like the beautiful sea
Your hands smooth like a baby touch
Honey I love you very much

Thank You

This is my thank you letter
To my Father for helping me to get better
This is my thank you letter
For letting me see the sunshine
I speak for all the sick, lame, and blind
This is a thank you letter for every time
You bless us when we pray
This is a thank you letter for the gifts you give
To my Father for letting me live
This is my thank you letter
For picking us up when we fall
This is a thank you letter
For all my family and friends
When we all think about it
You will send for us all in the end
From your daughter Robin and all other things
Lord teach me how to earn my wings
Thank you Lord Jesus for being a friend
Thank you Lord for forgiving sins
Thank you Lord we have won
We all want to hear well done
This is my thank you letter
Robin Anderson

The American Way

So many have made mistakes
So much a man can take
We live we multiply
We kill we die
We hurt we suffer
We fight over color
All these wars do
We know the truth
Families are far apart
Times are hard
We need one another
We still disc our sisters, and brothers
Fathers need their strength
Mothers go the extra length
Our families go to war
Our brothers and sisters in prison
They always hide when
They make wrong decisions
Some are guilty, some innocent
The innocent are killed
The guilty get away
I never understood any of this
I will continue to pray
Lord Jesus helps us in everyway
The Game
You play games on people brain
Making them think they are insane
You go out with your so called friends
You just got paid friends waiting

Your kids at home stomach aching
You sit on the corner wondering
What is your woman/man thinking?
Money gone you're not strong
In this game millions in fame
Hit that pipe it's all a game
One day you turn your key
In your house dealers are saying
Pay us our fee
It's all in the game
Times have really changed

The Lord Set Me Free

The Lord set me free
How can I repay thee?
I was in pain for years
The Lord came and wiped my tears
All of around the world
I speak for the little boys and girls
I love the Lord for what he's done
My victory is all in one
The Lord Jesus will set you free
Like he has done for me

The Lord

The Lord is good
The Lord is great
The Lord is powerful
The Lord is strong
The Lord will never
Leave you alone
Even when we are wrong
The feeling is real so real
I tell you this
He says love everyone
You do this and
All of your blessings will come

The Pack

A pack of wolves
A pack of sorrow
A pack of haters
A pack of destroyers
A pack of demons
A pack of folly
Take the pack of wolves
Turn it into love endures
Take the pack of sorrow
Live for this day not tomorrow
Take the pack of haters and
Pray that we all stand
At the city gate
Take the destroyers
And enjoy your little boy or girl
Take the pack of demons
Turn into god's stinger
Take the pack of folly
Turn it into jolly

The Road

The road out there is very hard
Not standing on corners
Not to disrespect
Not to fight
Not to kill
This kind of road is not the way
Kids listen to your parents
We do our best to keep you safe
The road is don't be anyone's fool
The road is stay in school
We should stay on the right road
Not what we want
Do what you are told
Let's stay on God's road

The World

What's the world about?
Why are we here
We know that Jesus is near
Families breaking up
Kids get pregnant
At a young age
Dad's leave them stuck
Politics, governments and
Violence in the streets
Homeless on every corner
24 hours a day
Instead of building shelters
They take them away
Millions of dollars
Building bridges and highways
This whole economic
Is just not right
How can work
If there are any jobs
How can we educate
If we cannot afford it
How can we love if we
Don't know what love is
What a world

Troubles Don't Last Always

Who said troubles last always
Some last for days and days
Some last for years and years
When trouble come our way
What do we say?
Some of us think that it's ok
Some think that trouble is here to stay
When God send for us
That's when our troubles go away
Troubles don't last always

Uncles

My uncles were very nice
I miss them a lot
They always told me
The right way to go
I did not listen at times
Some were just mean
Some let out a lot of steam
Some were a mess
All of them loved us
You could not tell if
They were under stress
They laughed and hurt like
All of us do
I tell you love your uncles
Today and always

Ups and Downs

When you're down
Where are your friends?
When you're down it seems
No one cares
When you're down where
Is your family
When you're down
Where is anyone
You be hoping someone
Would call or come
When you're down
Who cares for you?
When you're down
You're feeling the blues
When you come up in all
Your pennies here comes folks
Saying do I have any
When you're up here come folks
You have not seen in years
Knocking at your door crying tears
Telling you what they been
Through for years
It don't matter whether
You're up or down
That's just life you see
So why should it matter to me

Walk With Me Lord

Walk with me Lord
I don't know how
Walk with me Lord
Only you can feel
What I feel inside
Walk with me Lord
Every step of the way
When I walk alone
My steps go astray
Walk with me Lord
Guide my feet
I can't stand hell's heat
Walk with me Lord
Walk with me

Robin Anderson

Water Waves

It's nice to sit by the lake
And watch the pretty waves
Waves of joy
Waves of peace
Waves of laughter
Waves of love
Waves of friendship
Waves of the world
Waves of all the boys and girls

We All

It all happened to fast
I'm glad we all saw you
We had no idea
You were feeling blue
We all had our ups
We all had our downs
We will miss you not being around
Whatever the situation was
We all need to feel loved
Rest on our love one
Your pain your sadness is done
We will all remember your kind ways
The Lord kept you with us for days
No one knows when their time will come
We can't run and run
I tell you all this
God has us all on his list
Our Lord Jesus said come in
And suffer no more
I say to all my family and friends
We do not know when our life will end
If you do not Jesus
I just gave you some of the reasons
God Bless and be blessed to all
We Are
Women of power
Women of peace
Women of justice
Women of courage

Women of love
Women of expertise
One day one hour
Our love full of power
We are not of coldness
We are women of boldness
What such courage in us
One hand one chance
We are women of power

We Don't Have Many Days or Hours

We don't have many days
We should count every second or hours
It's God's love and his power
We don't have many days
We are caught up in
Our own selfish ways
We don't have many hours
We must understand
This is God's world not ours
Everyone wants their day
Everyone wants their hour
How can you make a strong tree sour?
You must be strong to stand like a flower
We don't have many days
We don't have many hours
We have to remember
This is God's world not ours

We Need to Hear

We need to hear
How are you today
We never know when
Jesus will come our way
We need to hear I love you
Today and everyday
To all my family and friends
I pray for the sick and the blind
We need to hear
I pray for your healing and
Have a blessed life
We need to hear
I say to the young and old
I love you today and always
Please don't give up your fight
He loves us day and night

What's A Person to Do?

What's a person to do?
No matter how hard you try
Here comes another person
Bringing tears to their eyes
As long as things are going their way
They don't have a word to say
What's a person to do?
When man makes them feel low
That's when some people say you're slow
What's a person to do?
When they are hurt
Some folks make them feel like dirt
My friends keep your head up
There is no such thing is good luck

What is a Pastor?

A pastor is someone
You look up to
A pastor is someone
Who comforts you?
A pastor is someone
Who teach the word?
A pastor is some
Who needs to be heard?
A pastor is someone
You can talk to
Go to a pastor when
You are feeling blue
Ladies, kids, and gents
We must understand
Sometimes a pastor needs
A helping hand
Pastor's have a life
Just like we do
When it comes to God
I believe all pastors should be true
We can't judge or say bad things
I don't say this to be mean
When it comes to pastors and everyone
Our Lord Jesus will say well done
What It Takes
It takes a strong man
It takes a strong woman
To stand by that strong man
It takes love

It takes pain
It takes peace
It takes sorrow
It takes joy
It takes up
It takes downs
It takes guidance
It takes power
It takes two to stand
All in one

What Must I Do

What must I do?
To keep loving you
What must I do?
I must give each day
For God let me live
I am a living testimony
I could have been dead and gone
He said Robin it's not
Your time to come home
Why we can't love and give
Thank the Lord everyday
He let us live

When I Fall

When I fall don't laugh
When I fall build me up
When I fall pray for me
When I fall help me see
When I fall Jesus help thee
When I fall I get back up
The Lord will fill my cup

When in Need

When in need put
Your pride aside let
The Lord be your guide
When in need go and pray
This I know Jesus will
Come your way
When in need don't say
I don't need anyone
The person you say
I don't need will be
The one who comes
This will be the person who cares
When it's all said and done

Who Am I?

Who am I?
Where do I come from?
Where do I walk?
Where do I stand?
Where is the promise land?
Where do we go?
Where is all the hope?
What makes me angry?
What makes me cry?
What makes me feel?
That I want to die
What shoes do you wear?
What pain do you bear?
Why do you look down at me?
What colors do you see?
Lift me up
Don't put me down
My feet still walk
On this old ground
Where do you come from?

Why Say

Why say love everyone if
It's not in your heart
Why say I'm hurt
When you give the pain
Why say help me
When you don't help yourself
Why you always want to receive
When you don't give
Why speak out before you think
You are hurting other people
What goes up must come down
The Lord gives and
The Lord takes away

Why So Much Pain

Lord why so much pain
I can't bare this pain alone
Help us Lord Jesus
You have showed us
What is to come?
Where do all this hurt?
Where does it really come from?
I want to thank you
For loving me so much
For putting up with me
For taking all of my pain
When my family and friends
Laugh at me no matter what it is
No matter what I do
You are there I know
I'm your child
Thank you for protecting us
In time of danger
For letting me see another day
Thank you for always coming my way

Why

Why are we here
What gifts to we have
Why so much killing
Why so much pain
What do you have to gain?
Why do kids hurt their parents?
Why do parents hurt their kids?
Why hurt me and say
I don't deserve to live
You are hurting your own
What consequence do you face?
Why kill one another over
Color creed or race
What happened to the dream?
So much blood shed
No reason at all
You will never know
When it's your call
Why take my life and
You don't feel a thing
Does it bother your conscious?
Do you want your wings?
Why look at me because
I have on wrong color clothes
I have on yellow, blue, or white
We are all precious in God sight
Stop fighting for what's wrong
And fight for what's right
Darkness is dark
Light is bright
Why sit and plan my death and
It could be yours this night
Stop the Violence

Wonder Why

I look at the clouds in the sky
I often wonder why
The wind blowing in different directions
Some of us can't be corrected
You go look for trouble
It comes back on you double
We can't go on this way
It hurts I don't know
If you are going to stay
I keep on moving anyway

You Bought Me Flowers

I was hoping for roses
You bought me pain
I was hoping for a white lily
You bought me suffering
I was hoping for a gardenia's
You bought me shame
I was hoping for a tulip
You bought me tears
I was hoping for an iris
You bought me darkness
When I am gone
Don't give me flowers

You don't Know Me

You don't know me
We are family
I have not heard from you
You don't know me
You hate me because of
What you hear and see
You don't know me
I pray you could
You will know I love you
With all my heart like Jesus would
You don't know me
I tried to make peace
You turned your back and waved your hand
I did all I can
We all have to be one
To get to the promise land

You Know Me

You know me
I pray for your healing
You know me
I love all of you
You know me
I am with you always
I walk, pray, and guide you
You can't see me
I see you
I feel your hurt and pain
You know me
When you are down
I pick you up
You know me
I am all I am
I am your Father
Your Lord and Savior

You Said

You said I won't hurt you
You said I won't leave
You said I love you
You hurt me and left
You left me by myself
You said I'm your star
You left me and
We are far apart
You said to this day
I say keep going
It's not going to work anyway

If I call you, it's to say I love you. If you have not heard from me, Remember you are always in my heart. I have no idea what you are going through…. or what pain you may have. Please do not look at me because of my face expressions. It may not be what you think or see. My words may seem scrambles at times. I mean no harm.

If I am hurting I do not want you to hurt. You may be hurting more than me And I do not want to put my burden on you. Whatever struggle or pain you may have, I pray that our Lord Jesus will touch and heal you. Remember I Love You. To all my family, friends, prosperity, peace, and healing to you all.

I would like to thank all of you who took your precious time out to read my book. Eugene, Edward thanks for your support in my deepest heartaches, when some laughed at me, called me dumb, stupid. Drexell thanks for coming into my life and given me laughter of joy, I really needed it at that time. Richard thanks, we had ups and downs. We all change at some point at in our lives.

If I say thanks a trillion times it would not be enough for what he has done for me. I could have been dead and gone our Lord Jesus, my Father kept me here, to all my brothers and sisters in Christ let your light shine, please stop the violence on our children, etc.

"Love is not an option, love is a need." (Quote)

I Am Human

You may think I am strong
I am weak and
I am only human
I make mistakes sometimes
Please forgive me
I am only human
I am not perfect
I have no more or less
I love everyone
Everyone will not love me back
I am only human
All I have been through
Our Lord Jesus loves me
He created me, he knows me
I am only human

I Arose

The stars in the night
My heart broken again
My eyes cry when it rains
I ask the Lord why so much pain
I want to fly and be free
When you seem so far away
I love you always
My hands are warm and true
You left me feeling blue
Where do we go from here?
I know the shepherd is near
I arose and it was he
I arose and
I'm free to be me

I Gave My All

I gave my all just
To take a fall
You told me where we stand
We don't have a second chance
The chance you had you blew it
You broke my heart
All the way through
I'll get back up no matter
What you say or do
Never again will
I fall for you
I gave my all

I Look

I look at the clouds in the sky
And I often wonder why
The wind blowing in different directions
Some of us can't be corrected
We go and look for trouble
It comes back double
We can't go on this way
It hurts I don't know if
You are going to stay
I keep on going anyway

I Say

You judge me by what you hear
No proof just the law
I say I'm innocent
You say I'm guilty
Some use their authority because
They have the power
The good suffer with the bad
Racism exist to this day
Let's face it
It's not going away
Jesus said in his word
They persecuted me
The will do you the same
Help us Lord keep us safe
All this war, all this hate
Help me Lord to redeem myself
Rescue me set me free
I said my innocent
I said my plea
Oh help us Lord, Jesus
I pray to thee

I Sit

I sit in my window
And look at the sky
I say Lord my, my
I sit in my chair
And think about our love ones
Most of them are gone
I see a beautiful rainbow
At the end of it is
A pot of God's gold
I sit by my window and see
The birds free
I say Lord help me please

I Stood Alone

I stood alone
A vision went across my eyes
I was so hurt
Never understood or questioned
All I know I became wise
I stood alone
I had a lot of love around me
Don't go to sleep angry
In peace stand alone
Sometimes in what you do stand alone
Whatever you have been through
Stand alone
We are not alone because
Our Lord Jesus
Stands with you

I Talked

One day in the early morning
My eyes felt stormy
I went to my prayer closet
I begin to open my mouth
I talked with Jesus
I cried unto him
He went to the Father
After I prayed I didn't feel bothered
He bought me out of a situation
I prayed with all my heart and soul
He gave me conformation
I want to thank you Lord
For all you have done
I shouted victory, victory
I have won

I Think

I think of you night and day
For every star in the sky
I imagine you go by
For every flower
That grows each day
I pray for you in everyway
For every tree that stand
I know you are a good man
For every step I take
I know you are my mate

About the Author

I was born May 30, 1963 to Lenora and Melvin Anderson, both are deceased. I have six brothers two, sisters, two brother-in-laws, and three sister-in-laws. Andrew deceased, Ronald, Melvin, (Gilva) David, (Trina) Richard, Robert (Vickie) Cheryl (Edward) ....and Lenora (Dwayne). We grew up in 4555 S Federal known to our family and friends as 55. Everyone was welcome in the Anderson home. We all were one big family on 45th street. I love you all it's too many of you to name.

I have four children. Melvin, Robin, Richard Jr., Lashell, one daughter-in-law Rosalind, 12 grandchildren and 4 that are not biologically mine, Sameka, Tameka, Chiquita, and you will always have a part in my life.

This book is dedicated to all who have been through….. heartaches, abuse, sufferings, etc.

Printed in the United States
By Bookmasters